GW01315952

Fear of Gambling Addiction Recovery

Holly Anne Ellison

Square Reads

ISBN 978-1-7391181-0-5

First edition

Contents

Free Offer   IV

Preface   V

Introduction   IX

1. We Don't Know What We Don't Know   1

2. Fear of the Unknown   7

3. You Will Stop Gambling   17

4. What Are You Afraid Of?   25

5. The Other Side of Addiction   33

6. Faith Over Fear   39

Conclusion   45

Thank You   51

References   52

Free Offer

To thank you for reading this book, I'm offering my PRE GAMBLING QUESTIONS Recovery Tool for **free**.

For **instant access** go to: www.squarereads.com

If you're serious about overcoming your gambling addiction, please take advantage of this special offer today to help you:

- Focus on What's Really Important to YOU

- Reinforce Your Commitment to Your Gambling Addiction Recovery

- Have a Barrier to Help You When Your GAM Strikes

Preface

I press the button. I dare not breathe. As the reels spin, I can feel the blood coursing through my veins. Inside I am trembling. This is my last push of the button. I have no more funds on my card. All the money I have loaded onto my card has gone. I only have enough for one more spin of the reels, at minimum bet. This is my last opportunity to have a win. I desperately need it to turn around.

And then the reels stop.

Nothing.

As much as I can't believe it, I can. I am not surprised. With each press of the button, I felt it was going nowhere, yet I had still continued.

Really!

After everything I've put in, *you take it all.* I feel total disgust. Not sure who this is directed at. The casino, the slot machine, myself?

I sit for a few seconds. Thoughts running through my head. Can I get more money? Should I? Suddenly I find myself asking the person next to me to watch my slot machine while I go to the cashier. I do the walk of shame, again.

This is my third time today. I have already reached my daily ATM withdrawal limit so have no choice but to go to the casino cashier.

I find myself standing in the queue. Every part of me is willing myself to step out of the line. Run. Go home. But I don't move, except to shuffle forward as the queue to the cashier slowly moves.

I tell myself this is wrong. I've already lost so much. But there's another voice in my head, much louder than my own that is encouraging me, telling me it will all work out. One more press of the button. One more spin of the reels and I could get everything back. I could even win big. I listen to that voice.

After all, it has been right before!

It's my turn at the cashier desk. I hand over my bank card and ask for a withdrawal. Does she know how much I've already spent today? I feel so embarrassed, but still, I proceed with the transaction. The funds are loaded to my casino card. Relief. I'm back in business.

I stop at the bar on the way back and get a glass of wine. Now the fun is going to start.

I have my drink, money on my card, and my favorite slot machine waiting for me. This is a fresh start.

I sit down. Insert my card. Take a sip of wine, press that button, and pray.

And so another session of **madness** begins.

Introduction

"The oldest and strongest emotion of mankind is fear, and the oldest and strongest kind of fear is fear of the unknown" **- H. P. Lovecraft**

YOU'VE PROBABLY TRIED TO get over your gambling addiction before. And despite your good intentions and best effort, you never managed to free yourself.

Could fear of recovery be what's holding you back?

You may think this a strange question, but I want you to give it some consideration.

There are many factors that contribute to one person enjoying harmless fun in the casino occasionally and others who start this way, who end up as addicted gamblers. As an addicted gambler, you've probably heard all the theories before.

It's in the genes so you are predisposed to addiction. You are an adrenalin junkie in constant need of your next fix. You are depressed and just want to escape. Personally, I don't believe it is any one thing, but rather a combination of circumstances, feelings, and financial ability. Some factors are more dominant and contribute more to the start of the problem.

Over time we don't even think about this. We have turned the corner and gambling is not just fun anymore. It has become a compulsion.

Of course, there are a combination of factors that enabled us to become addicted to gambling, and so too are there many recovery options for us to take advantage of with the goal of overcoming our addiction. However, many don't work in isolation, and often a combination of methods, thoughts, attitudes, and practical steps are necessary for a successful recovery.

But no matter what we try, if our frame of mind isn't in the right place, nothing will work.

Our foundation has to be solid. No cracks. What we are doing is life-changing. We have to be able to count on it and need the effort that we put in to be worth it. We need to be able to see results. We need to be able to feel the change and trust that we are doing the right thing and finally, it is all going to work out.

No more false hope and broken promises. Let's do this right!

You've tried before, probably numerous times, but you've never quite gotten there.

I understand. Fear got you first!

It's strange to think that something you want to do - something that will benefit you for the rest of your life, could be ruined because of fear.

When most people think of fear it is about something that is dangerous or potentially harmful. People can be afraid of a variety of things, some being quite reasonable and common, whilst other fears are irrational and experienced by only a few.

My name's Holly Anne Ellison and it's my goal to help as many compulsive gamblers recover from their gambling addiction as possible, today. I am not a psychologist, nor a trained counselor. What I bring to the table is my own decades-long gambling addiction and the solutions and understanding that finally worked for me for good which I will discuss briefly in this short book.

For many years gambling was my nemesis. I was addicted to playing casino slots, specifically certain slot games. Not only was I obsessed with the game, but with the actual slot machine in the casino. It became "my" slot machine.

The thought of arriving at the casino to find another player on that machine was unbearable.

As I would wait for the machine to become available, the possibility of that person playing on "my" machine and winning it big was a real fear to me.

Instead of just having fun and enjoying myself somewhere else in the casino, I would hover and wait for "my" machine to become available.

Yes, I was that person!

I was probably the worst addicted slots player. What started out as a fun pastime, over time, evolved into something far worse. Gambling took over my life. It drained my finances and strained my relationships. Every waking moment was filled with casino thoughts, replaying when I last went and anticipating my next visit.

It was no longer fun. It became who I was. What I did. What I had to do.

I learned affiliate marketing so I could generate extra funds specifically to fund my gambling habit.

And even with knowing the negative impact it was having on my life, I could not stop. For years I continued down that path, spiraling out of control.

Being a gambling addict was just who I was. Of course, initially, I had denied this, not only to others but to myself. I made up all sorts of reasons as to why I gambled. I justified my behavior however I could.

I was trapped in a place of my own creation. But what was the alternative?

Although I didn't want to throw any more money away or deal with the strong urge to gamble anymore and the inevitable internal battles that would always ensue, to give up gambling would be like giving up part of myself.

And often the quickest way to end the battle would be to just give in and gamble, even though I really didn't want to. I often just found myself gambling without the desire to do so. I was automated. I wasn't me.

This may sound like an excuse to some, but it was a very important clue that I used to formulate my own gambling addiction recovery plan.

I am happy to say I finally discovered a way out. I did this completely on my own without any support.

I overcame my fear of giving up gambling, a fear I didn't realize I had until one day it hit me. With that realization, everything changed. Something changed within me, and I suddenly felt in control again. I felt free. I was free.

But why had it taken me so long?

Chapter One

We Don't Know What We Don't Know

"Without knowledge action is useless and knowledge without action is futile." - Abu Bakr

ONE DAY I WAS shopping with my three-year-old granddaughter. We were in a clothing store and I was looking for something to wear on our upcoming holiday. I selected a few items and told my granddaughter I would try them on.

The look of horror on her face was so unexpected.

"You can't take off your clothes in the store!" she exclaimed. "The people will laugh at you."

She was being quite serious. I quickly reassured her that was not my intention and that we would go to the dressing rooms to try on the clothes. I held her hand and led her to the back of the store where the dressing rooms were located.

We entered the cubicle and she stood there totally surprised, hands-on-hips, and innocently asked me, "How did you know about this?"

Of course, being only three she had not yet experienced going to dressing rooms to try on clothes in the store. All her clothes were bought off the rack using age as a guideline. As this was not in her life experience, she had no idea that this was what people did.

And nor should she have.

But it raised an interesting point for me. As adults, we think we know a lot about life and how the world works, but what if we only think we do. What if we too, don't know what we don't know?

I knew with my own gambling addiction recovery that not everything I had tried had worked for me and I guessed this was probably true for others too. Something was always missing. While trying different things, I too didn't know what I didn't know, yet.

In my quest for recovery, I grasped everything I had been told about gambling. I knew what was expected of me. I understood the reaction I was supposed to have when given the knowledge that was supposed to cure me. However, this wasn't the case. Although I heard and understood what was being said, it didn't reach the place within me that would be able to make sense of it and take action.

And in those days, I really *didn't* know what I know today. I didn't even know that I didn't know it, because you don't know what you don't know, until of course, you do.

Please take a moment to think about that.

Quite by accident, I experienced something really positive in my life. I had done something successfully that I had been afraid to do and with that came emotions that I had not felt in decades. In fact, it had been so long ago, that I didn't even know I could feel that way.

My daughter had been encouraging me for ages to start an Instagram account for an online store I was working on. The thought of this terrified me.

It seemed that Instagram was very different from Facebook in that you had to follow a certain form, brand identity, and color scheme to get the chance for lots of engagement. You also had to depend more on your phone to manage this which I was extremely uncomfortable with.

I kept putting this off. I dabbled in creating the right look and the longer I dabbled, the more successful I was in delaying the inevitable. I accept that to some of you this may sound rather silly, especially to those of you who use Instagram and social media a lot, but to me, at that time, it was all quite overwhelming.

Anyway, with my daughter's help, I finally created my business Instagram account and it took off. In a relatively short time, I had thousands of followers with a pretty good engagement.

This was totally unexpected and in hindsight, it had been very easy to do. The fears I felt before taking the plunge were all in my head and the reality was actually very different.

This realization was a real eye-opener and another clue to my path of recovery. I finally felt like there was hope and saw the light at the end of the tunnel.

From that venture, I realized that I had a fear of change and the unknown. I was hiding from myself in the darkness of being boxed into my gambling addiction.

Somehow there was security in the insecurity of my compulsive gambling. I was comfortable with the discomfort I experienced from the continued manipulation of my finances. I was able to endure the stress of hiding my deceit from others, and more importantly, from myself.

At least that is what I thought I was doing. But of course, the stress was not only having an impact on my mental health, but it was also presenting physical symptoms too. I was overweight and had developed Type 2 Diabetes and getting a good night's sleep was a rarity.

With this realization that I was actually more afraid of what life would become if I wasn't a gambler, came more thought. I suddenly found myself thinking deeply about everything. Being in my mid-fifties at the time added a sense of urgency to sort myself out once and for all, in all areas of my life.

The clock was ticking.

I knew if I didn't make a big change and confront my fear now, this was going to be me for the rest of my life. I would permanently be stuck living the life of somebody I didn't like. I had already wasted so much time.

Time to make something of myself, to feel really good about me, was not on my side.

I knew I wanted to be able to look at myself in the mirror and acknowledge, at the very least, that I had given it a damn good try.

It was time to take back my life. It was time for me to formulate a plan drawing on all my previous experience and knowledge.

I now knew what I hadn't known before. And because I finally understood that fear had been my obstacle all the time, I could now face it and confront it head-on.

When you have a different challenge to overcome, you can go about it differently, and as you make inroads into that new challenge, the ability to do the same with your gambling addiction is affected positively.

Overcoming my fear of change, fear of failure, and fear of being myself was the first step I took on my own recovery journey. Before you know it, one step leads to two and you have momentum.

But you first have to start your journey with that first single step!

Chapter Two

Fear of the Unknown

"If we fear the unknown then surely, we fear ourselves." - **Bryant H. McGill**

FEAR OF THE UNKNOWN can also be masking fear of change. As humans, we take comfort in the familiarity of routine, even when we know it is not in our best interests.

Not knowing the outcome of a situation can be scary. Often, we don't know that we suffer from this, but by examining our behavior, we can see that our gambling addiction may be rooted in fear of the unknown.

We remain rooted where we are because we are not able to see what can be. Whilst some people embrace the opportunity to explore the unknown, the very thought of opening the door and permanently shutting it behind them as they venture into the unknown is overwhelming.

According to Lydia Antonatos of Choosing Therapy, "*People who are overpowered by a fear of change are more likely to cope by avoiding new situations. They often lack interest in exploring new things and may be reluctant to achieve goals or improve their situation. They even might find themselves stuck in toxic relationships or jobs they don't like, which can bring about stress, anxiety, pain, depression, and a lack of energy.*" (Antonatos, 2022)

If we look at the compulsive gambler more closely, many of the characteristics mentioned above about fear of change are present. Sometimes we don't want to acknowledge them and are in complete denial that something is wrong, or we know something is wrong but don't understand the hold it has on us.

We avoid new situations and stick to the familiar casino(s) and even the same casino games. We are not interested in doing anything else and when we do, we just go through the motions as our head is usually filled with thoughts of how we would rather be gambling instead. We may have goals to improve our finances if possible, with the main motivation being to finance our gambling addiction rather than improving our lives overall.

Maybe some parts of our lives are going well which makes us deny there is any issue at all, however, issues generally don't affect one area only and the negativity will spill over into other parts too.

When you are fearful of one situation, this does not necessarily mean you are a fearful or scared person in general. On the contrary, you may demonstrate the ability to act fearlessly in many situations and this is easy because when you do this you are not acting out of fear.

"Lack of predictability and control can be contributing factors to fear. If little information is available to predict an outcome or make a decision, this can increase feelings of anxiety and uncertainty." (Stuck, 2022)

I find it extremely interesting that the factors that contribute to fear like lack of predictability and control are the same factors that compulsive gamblers continually experience and live with.

As we are already experiencing these, on some level, is it just too much to add more of this into our lives by changing and dealing with the fear of the unknown, that we remain firmly planted in our gambling misery?

The problem arises when action is needed that involves overcoming a fear first.

And of course, it's impossible to overcome a fear that you don't even know you have.

Most of the time we are completely aware of our fears, fear of heights, fear of spiders, fear of flying. Once you identify your fear, you can take the steps to overcome it.

If you suspect that perhaps you do have a fear of the unknown, you can do something about it.

1. Get a New Perspective

2. Expect the Unexpected

3. Set Yourself Up for Success

4. Focus on the Whole

5. Take Action

Get a New Perspective

With a brand-new perspective comes a brand-new attitude. By trying to overcome your fears to deal with your gambling addiction recovery from the same perspective that created them, you are more likely to fail. I believe that is why so many compulsive gamblers relapse.

"Whatever recovery path they choose, about 90% of problem gamblers relapse, a slightly higher rate than for other types of addicts. This doesn't mean recovery is near impossible to achieve, says Hodgins, but indicates that addicts often make several attempts before they succeed."
(Collier, 2015)

The method that I found to be the most effective for me was to embody my future self. This was still me, but the best version of myself. My future self was everything my current self wanted to be.

She was confident, successful, and had peace of mind. Most importantly, she did not suffer from a gambling addiction and was able to make decisions in her best interest from a place of clarity.

This method was extremely helpful for two reasons. Firstly, by adopting the perspective of my future self, I was able to make better decisions and secondly, by creating her and getting to know her, I was eliminating the unknown. I knew who she was and once I knew that, I simply had to formulate a plan to ensure I really became her.

In addition, I was able to separate my gambling addiction from myself. In other words, my addiction was not me, but rather something that resided in me, which I named my GAM, *Gambling Addiction Monster*.

Expect the Unexpected

Most journeys worth taking are not the direct path between two points. They include detours to beautiful scenery, opportunities to meet interesting people, and can reinforce your joy in life.

The same can be said for your recovery. It probably won't be straightforward so don't expect it to be so. By mentally preparing for unexpected challenges, you will be better prepared to cope with them. Don't let them derail you but rather look at them as opportunities to prove how far you've come.

When you overcome obstacles or unexpected life challenges, your confidence in your own abilities will be heightened resulting in an overall positive boost to your general welfare.

Set Yourself Up for Success

With all the money and time you are going to save as you make progress in your recovery, you need to find something to do that will make you feel like a true winner in life.

Your something can be anything you would like it to be but has to be something that will make you feel good and excited to get out of bed each day.

It all depends on your interests; this could be taking up charity work, signing up for a course, getting more involved in a hobby you've dabbled in, starting a side-hustle, or opening a business.

Create something positive for yourself by investing your time, money, and energy where the outcome depends on you and what you do and not the roll of a dice or press of a button.

Putting as much effort and thought into this as you did into your gambling will pay off; and when it does, it will all be down to you. This will be a genuine win for you, a win that you can maintain and build upon.

Focus on the Whole

In order to be the best version of yourself, you need to focus on the whole of yourself. As well as adjusting your mindset, you need to take action to look after your physical health and connect with your spiritual side too.

Remember your body has been conditioned to associate gambling with the release of dopamine. So when the dopamine craving takes hold, you are compelled to satisfy that urge the only way you know how.

"When dopamine is released in large amounts, it creates feelings of pleasure and reward, which motivate you to repeat a specific behavior." (Julson, 2022)

Dopamine can, however, be released into your system naturally and there are things that you can easily do to enhance this.

Attention should be given to your diet, exercise, and sleep patterns. By eating a balanced diet with high protein content, the dopamine levels in your system will be raised naturally. Even eating a bar of chocolate can make a difference.

"Though chocolate is known for its ability to increase levels of the calming neurotransmitter serotonin, it also contains small amounts of a compound called phenylethylamine, which acts like an amphetamine, stimulating your brain cells to release dopamine." (Roizman, 2018)

A good night's sleep and even moderate exercise will have positive benefits. All in all, you need your body to be in harmony with your mind so that your thoughts are focused on what you really need to do instead of chasing that gambling high.

Take Action

Knowledge is power.

However, without action, knowledge is simply that, knowledge. Action is the ingredient that will turn your knowledge into a power that you can use to get your life back on track.

Don't procrastinate.

Start by setting goals that will propel you forward. Explore your options so you fully understand what you need to do. It's always good to be specific, so you can measure your progress rather than having a vague objective that can easily be forgotten or ignored.

The most important action you can do today is to put up as many barriers as you possibly can between you and your gambling addiction. This is probably the first obstacle you will experience and one that is crucial for your recovery.

Close your casino accounts.

It's that simple.

If you can do this today or when you next feel clear-headed, this will make all the difference. If you can't access the casino, you simply can't gamble.

You can also look for online support, get therapy, or sign up for a Gambling Recovery program.

It's time to be fearless.

Chapter Three

You Will Stop Gambling

"I got sober. I stopped killing myself with alcohol. I began to think: 'Wait a minute—if I can stop doing this, what are the possibilities?' And slowly it dawned on me that it was may be worth the risk." - **Craig Ferguson**

EVEN THOUGH THE ABOVE quote relates to alcoholism, the essence of the message conveys that giving up an addiction can be risky.

It's risky because you don't know what's on the other side of that addiction. You've become so used to being a compulsive gambler that you don't know how not to be one. It's who you are. You identify as a gambler.

Giving up parts of our identity can be tricky, even when we know it's what's best for us. But it doesn't have to be. Separating myself from my GAM was essential to my recovery.

The risk to your health and life when you continue with your addiction is far riskier.

You will give up being a gambler. You will not always live as one.

It can happen in one of three ways:.

>   1. Hitting Rock Bottom

>   2. Death by Suicide

>   3. Making a Conscious Decision

Hitting Rock Bottom

You know you don't want to be there. Believe me, you now have it good even though it might not feel like it. You may have problems, but you still have choices. If you're gambling, it's because you have the funds to do so. This doesn't mean you can afford to. It means you have access to funds that you are diverting to gambling.

When you hit rock bottom everything you have today will be gone. Your money, your self-respect, your ability to choose and even your relationships will become a memory.

And with every bet or push of the button, this day is coming closer.

The false hope that we get from the big wins that we experience on occasions perpetuates this self-destructive cycle. This has happened before so it can happen again. Sure it can, but how much do you have to lose before, and will the win be more than you've lost? Probably not. And what if that win never comes?

All the resources you have today to use to create a different life for yourself will no longer be available to you.

If you've felt guilt or shame before as a compulsive gambler, these feelings will only be amplified when you hit rock bottom. The overwhelming feeling of regret, together with the knowledge of being trapped in a reality that you could have avoided will be soul-destroying.

This is a regret you don't want to live with.

And unfortunately, some can't.

Death by Suicide

To put context into the severity of suicide in gambling, it is helpful for us to understand the growing number of problem gamblers in the USA. The number of people affected by this addiction has grown over time worldwide as the ability to access casinos and gambling sites online has increased.

"Applying these rates to the U.S. Census estimates of the number of residents age 18 or older in 1997 (196 million) indicates that currently about 1.8 million adults are pathological gamblers and 5.7 million are either pathological or problem gamblers." (National Research Council, 1999)

According to Colleen Jones of the Mid-Hudson Problem Gambling Resource Center: "*It has been found that 37% of those struggling with problem gambling and 49% of those with a pathological Gambling Disorder have suicidal ideations. Statistics also show that 17% of problem gamblers and 18% of those with a Gambling Disorder attempt suicide.*" (Jones, 2020)

These numbers are staggering. Clearly, suicide in gambling addicts is a huge problem that needs to be addressed. Two main factors contribute to the reasons why gamblers turn to suicide.

Firstly, they are still gambling and living with the constant need to satisfy an urge that they feel they can't control, which becomes too much. They are tired of the internal struggle, the shame, and the guilt. They can't deal with the enemy within anymore.

Life without peace of mind, sound judgment, and faith in oneself is not worth living. Many compulsive gamblers have often tried unsuccessfully to get over their addiction but reach the point where they can't see this ever happening and feel this is their only way out.

They just want it all to end.

Secondly, they are not gambling anymore because they finally reached rock bottom. Living with self-loathing, regret and shame is unbearable. Also now being without any resources of their own, they need to be dependent upon the kindness, understanding, and generosity of others, and this is not something they feel entitled to or worthy of, so they conclude that everybody would be better off without them.

What could be worse than the unnecessary end of a life that had so much potential because they couldn't see that the magic they sought so desperately outside of themselves, was always within?

Making a Conscious Decision

It is important to understand that people addicted to gambling do recover. They often do this completely on their own, without any treatment, as in the case of my own recovery.

"Pathological gambling may not always follow a chronic and persisting course. A substantial portion of individuals with a history of pathological gambling eventually recover, most without formal treatment." (Slutske, 2006)

Your recovery journey begins with the conscious decision to do everything in your power to overcome your addiction. It's imperative that you dig deep and tap into that part of you that is shouting out to be saved.

Use those same skills you have used over and over again to convince yourself gambling is a good idea because now your life really does depend on it.

Sometimes the thought of something is worse than the reality.

Have you often delayed doing something as simple as washing the dishes because the thought of it was too much? So you sat there unnecessarily surrounded by dirty dishes all day and when you finally got to do them, it was easier than you had anticipated and you wondered why you hadn't just dealt with it earlier.

So don't put off committing to this decision. Decide today and then follow through with everything you need to do to ensure your success.

In order to make the conscious decision to stop gambling and overcome the fears you may have, you need to explore any fears that could possibly be hindering your recovery.

- Are you afraid of what a gambling-free future could look like?

- Are you afraid of an unknown future?

- Are you afraid to make changes?

- Are you afraid of commitment?

- Are you afraid of facing the underlying cause of your addiction?

- Are you afraid that you simply won't know what to do?

- Do you fear discovering that after gambling, you still don't amount to anything?

- Do you worry that giving up gambling won't be everything it's cracked up to be?

- Are you afraid of facing other realities in your life when your method of escape is no longer an option?

These are simply ideas. Only you know what your fear could possibly be and it's up to you to consider your own thoughts on the above ideas and look within to find your own fear that is preventing you from a permanent recovery.

Chapter Four

What Are You Afraid Of?

"Every worthy act is difficult. Ascent is always difficult. Descent is easy and often slippery." - **Mahatma Gandhi**

Now it's time to explore what's been holding you back from your gambling addiction recovery.

Life can be extremely difficult right now for most people and the pressure on those with an addiction can be even more so. Our world can sometimes feel like a scary place because we are having to face and deal with issues that most have not had to confront before.

The world today as we used to know it doesn't exist. For the first time, we have had to experience life through a worldwide pandemic and more recently, the possibility of a worldwide war.

However we view fear of the unknown, or fear of change, we've had no choice but to just go with it. Covid-19 lockdowns and wearing masks became normal and for a period the possibility of death was very real.

Changes were forced upon us which we legally had to comply with. We had no choice in the matter and although these changes were difficult and often uncomfortable, we adapted and survived.

It's now time for *you* to make the changes in your life that are needed for your mental health and survival.

So, what are you really afraid of?

There are three possible fears that you could experience.

     1. Fear of Giving Up What Could Be

     2. Fear of Not Being Worthy or Good Enough

     3. Fear of Facing Underlying Issues

Fear of Giving Up What Could Be

Do you have more faith in the ability to win big in a casino than to do something big for yourself where you depend only upon your own abilities to do so? Casinos need you and your money to achieve their goals. They don't care about you. You are simply a means to an end.

They will provide the illusion of care by offering free drinks, meals, accommodation, and gaming credits. When we receive these, we feel special and privileged, but there is nothing special about it. This is just what casinos do to keep their players depositing money to fill their own coffers.

You need to consider why you have more faith in a casino whose only goal is to make a profit from you, than faith in your own abilities.

If you give up gambling today, do you feel that you could possibly be giving up on that elusive big win that you've been playing for all these years? I used to believe that one day I too would win it big. I had seen others experience these mega life-changing wins and expected that one day it would be my turn.

When you give up this dream, you may feel that you are giving up the possibility of ever experiencing that kind of luck and good fortune. If you don't get it from the casino, where else are you going to get it?

A big win would not only be financially rewarding but would be confirmation that you are special, as this experience is only for a very rare group of people and you want to be part of that group.

You have been conditioned to expect that big win for so long. Every internal argument you have had with yourself has included this possibility and to simply walk away and give up on something you have invested so much time and money in can be frightening.

So to give up this particular dream feels like giving up on the future you have envisioned for yourself for so long.

This is not exactly what you have to do. With a shift of perspective, you can formulate a new dream, a dream that you have control over.

I know that too may seem overwhelming, but believe me, it is not as overwhelming as the casino roller coaster ride. And if you have been able to handle that, this will be a walk in the park.

It's time to face the fact that if you were going to win really big, you would have done so by now. And on the off chance you are one of those few that achieved this, why are you still gambling? Do you believe lightning will strike twice? And how much of that money has already been put back into gambling, chasing another big win?

The moment one door closes, another one opens. You already know that being a gambling addict is not in your best interests. You already know that you want something better for yourself.

And you should.

You deserve it.

By giving up gambling permanently, you are creating space for something new, something better, something that will enhance your life where you will get to feel those feelings you have been chasing.

Fear of Not Being Worthy or Good Enough

As unlikely as it is that you will experience a mega win in your lifetime, do you somehow feel that the odds of this happening are greater than achieving success in your own right?

Do you feel that success is for other people? You may already have a good career so may not feel the need to change this. And you don't have to.

Success means different things to different people. Some people associate success with material objects, others with personal accomplishments or simply feeling content and happy when they shut their eyes at night to go to sleep.

Everybody wants to feel inner peace, and this will never be achieved from gambling. Once you have put this behind you, your emotions and thoughts will stabilize and you can tap into the resources you have within to do whatever it takes to bring you joy.

This does not have to be scary. It's an exciting thing to look inside and see what's really there.

And believe me, something wonderful is there.

All the time you spent focused on chasing a pipe dream and feeding your addiction, made this incredible part of you smaller and smaller that you no longer felt its presence.

And when you don't feel you have it within you, you don't believe that you have what is needed to create your own success and happiness.

First of all, it's important to manage your expectations of yourself. Nobody would expect you to go from being a gambling addict to creating or achieving something phenomenal right away.

Just giving up gambling is an achievement all on its own and you need to celebrate and acknowledge this. If you can do this you have what it takes to achieve a lot more, once you have opened up space in your life for something else.

Comparing yourself to others is something you shouldn't do either as this can increase self-doubt. However, it is good to have a role model to emulate and learn from.

YouTube is full of creators sharing their content for free and is definitely worth exploring. You can find resources to learn a new skill which you can then implement to help your recovery. When you have a topic that grabs your interest, make sure you find the best person on that topic to learn from.

Fear of Facing Underlying Issues

Your gambling addiction has been a way of coping with problems in your life that you have not yet dealt with. In order for you to fully recover, it will be necessary for you to get to the root cause of your issue. This could be a problem that you don't want to think about that you've buried deep within yourself. Your gambling probably started off as a distraction only to become another problem you have to deal with.

You've been avoiding dealing with this underlying issue for so long, and although you know you will have to finally deal with it, the very thought of facing it can be terrifying. This is time for a lot of self-reflection. This doesn't mean being critical of yourself and focusing on the past. What's done is done.

Now is the moment for looking within, to look past any fears you may have, and to awaken the being within you that wants to step up to the challenge and make a difference.

The being inside who wants to be free of the madness.

Chapter Five

The Other Side of Addiction

"Though no one can go back and make a brand-new start, anyone can start from now and make a brand-new ending."
- Carl Bard

THERE ARE MOMENTS, HOURS, and even days sometimes where everything is clear and we don't feel the need to gamble. We might think about it, just like you might think about how you might want to go out for dinner to that new restaurant around the corner. There is no internal battle. You don't feel like you could tear your world apart at any minute. It's only a thought. You have peace of mind, and it feels great.

When you've finally put gambling behind you, this is how it always feels. You get to permanently enjoy the clarity and calm you experience in between those adrenaline-filled gambling episodes when the guilt has dissipated, and you feel in control of yourself again.

I am referring to the quiet before the storm, after you've made all sorts of promises to yourself, when you truly feel confident that next time will be different. Next time you will know better. Next time you won't give in.

Your intentions are so good. In these in-between moments, you truly believe that you've got a grip. Until there it is again. That urge. Calling you, pushing you, often completely out of the blue capturing you totally unaware.

And the battle with yourself begins again. You feel helpless and trapped. I know you do your best to fight it. You don't want to be a compulsive gambler. The internal argument doesn't ever end. You don't get the final word.

Almost like an out-of-body experience, you suddenly find yourself logging into your online casino account or getting in the car to go to the casino. On some level, you believe that this terrible feeling you are experiencing will disappear as soon as you start placing your bets or pushing that button. And you're right, for a short time it does.

If you're winning, you will tell yourself you've done the right thing. You will justify to yourself that what you're doing is right for you, this time. You will tell yourself you will take money home, this time. But before you know it, your winnings are disappearing, and the fun ride is over. It's time again for another internal battle.

Do you stay or do you go? Do you call it a day or do you get more money and continue playing?

And because you're a compulsive gambler you will make the choice that most people out for a fun night won't make. You will get more money from wherever you can. You will take it from the funds you have to live on for the month. You will take it from your credit cards. It doesn't matter.

You just need to continue because that internal conflict is just too much.

You're not thinking clearly. You're not thinking about the consequences. You're not really even thinking. Once again, you've become automated. You do the walk of shame to the ATM or cashier to get that money.

And this continues until you have no more money. When you have no more money, there is no more internal conflict because there is nothing to be conflicted about. It's all gone. You have no choice but to call it a day.

But you don't feel at peace. You feel sick to your stomach. You feel so guilty. You feel worthless. Once again, you've let yourself down. You've lied to yourself and probably others too. You don't like who you are.

You will feel like this for a day or two and then slowly these negative feelings will fade away to be replaced with false promises and confidence that you will never do that again.

Never!

But you will. It's all part of the cycle. You are an addicted gambler and this is your trip.

This is no way to live, for yourself and for those who you love and who love you. It certainly isn't good for your mental health and will have a negative impact on your physical well-being.

It's important to understand the physicality of what has been going on in your body; this will also provide some understanding as to why you gamble as you do.

Our bodies are full of hormones that all have a role to play in our existence. According to Algamus Gambling Treatment, *"Gambling triggers the brain's reward system which are linked primarily to the pleasure and motivation centers and releases dopamine into the body. This makes the gambler feel elated while they're putting it on the line and taking risks. Dopamine is the dominant power driver and the chief neurotransmitter in the reward system."* (Benson, 2018)

For a long time, you have lived with this yo-yo effect of dopamine craving and release into your body.

When you stop your compulsive gambling, you will no longer be subjected to these heightened effects and can potentially suffer gambling withdrawal systems.

It's good to know that dopamine can be released naturally into the system by choosing a good lifestyle so you can still feel good.

"Getting enough sleep, exercising, listening to music, meditating, and spending time in the sun can all boost dopamine levels. Overall, a balanced diet and lifestyle can go a long way in increasing your body's natural production of Dopamine and helping your brain function at its best."
(Julson, 2022)

What's done is done. You cannot change the past. You only have the power to change what you do from now on.

Imagine how good you will feel when you are no longer subjected to these extreme highs and lows of dopamine. Imagine how wonderful it will be when you naturally feel good without guilt or shame. Imagine what you could do with all the money you save. When you do not have to deal with conflict within yourself anymore, you will experience peace of mind that you have never felt before.

You will no longer only get to enjoy all the benefits of a gambling-free life in those in-between moments, but **every day**.

Imagine what you could do with that.

Chapter Six

Faith Over Fear

"You can come out of the furnace of trouble two ways: if you let it consume you, you come out a cinder; but there is a kind of metal which refuses to be consumed, and comes out a star." - **Jean Church**

YOU ARE THAT STAR.

You may not feel like it today, but if you've got this far in the book, you are definitely a step further to becoming the person you want to be.

Somewhere inside you, there's a voice that wants to be heard. It's now time to listen.

True recovery comes only when you do it for yourself. Although the benefits will impact others positively, you cannot get over an addiction to please other people or because you feel pressure from society.

Only you can do it, and you can only do it for yourself!

Every time I relapsed in my own recovery, I had undertaken that journey for the wrong reasons. I didn't understand the importance of the reason underlying the decision to stop gambling. I knew it was the right thing to do. I didn't want to waste money anymore and I was tired of feeling guilty and letting my family down.

And although all these reasons are good, they were more about running away from the consequences of gambling instead of running toward something more, something truly special and something that I could build upon.

I want to share a method that I found extremely helpful and to which I attribute part of my success in overcoming my own addiction recovery.

I had proved over and over again that I was not capable of making good choices or responsible behavior. My credibility with myself had long since been invalidated. My own thoughts were clouded with hard self-judgments, fear of failure, guilt, and pessimism.

Although the outside world saw a smile, I was a walking body of negativity.

A new perspective was required. Fresh thoughts were needed. A brand-new attitude was the order of the day.

I had to find a way of separating the old me, the me with all the issues, from the new me, the me I wanted to be. The me I knew I could be if I could only get over my addiction to gambling.

I had already made excellent progress with this concept before when I separated myself from my gambling addiction. By doing this it was far easier to win those ongoing internal battles that compulsive gamblers face every time the gambling urge arises. This concept is fully explained in my upcoming book *Gambling Addiction Monster*.

Don't get me wrong. It won't always be plain sailing. You will have days when you really have to dig deep but I know you are strong. You've been strong for years. You've just been applying your strength to the wrong things.

I entirely agree with the wise words in this Anne Fletcher quote, *"Nobody stays recovered unless the life they have created is more rewarding and satisfying than the one they left behind."* (Fletcher, 2022)

You have to believe you can make yourself a rewarding and satisfying life.

Instead of feeling excited about gambling, feel excited about creating the new you. Yes, I used the word create because that is what you're going to do. You need to start imagining your future self. First of all, she is not a gambler. She does not make excuses and is always up for a challenge even if the path ahead looks difficult.

She believes in herself. She knows she has so much life experience to draw upon. She taps into that experience and embraces opportunities. She is no longer afraid to be who she is.

She is confident in herself. She doesn't care what others think about her. What's important to her is what she thinks about herself. She likes what she sees in the mirror, especially the light back in her eyes.

She feels alive. She is not just existing between one gambling session and another, but actually has a life.

She uses her time wisely. She works hard and plays hard. Oh yes, just because she's given up gambling doesn't mean she's given up fun.

These are some of the qualities I saw in my future self that I used to finally get over my own gambling addiction. I am sure you will have your own. You know exactly what qualities your future self has. You know what's important to her, you know what she believes in, and you know what she needs from you.

Use this knowledge to create her. Give her the best parts of you. Connect with her emotionally. Show her the love and appreciation you've always wanted and see what you get back in return.

Trust me, if you do this, you won't be disappointed.

The sooner you get to know her, the better. You are going to hand over the reins of your life to her. Every decision from today should be made from the point of view of your future self because she is not weighed down by the past and is not capable of self-destructive behavior. She thinks clearly and will always do what's in her best interest.

And of course, what's in *her* best interest, is what's best for *you*. She lives in faith, not fear, and so can you!

And once you've put the fear behind you, you will be able to move into your new life. The feeling of calm in the knowing that your good intentions and actions will no longer be derailed by that uncontrollable urge will become your new normal. You will experience peace of mind in the ability to manage your finances correctly and will find pleasure in being able to shop for things that your gambling addiction has deprived you of for so long.

I can't stress how powerful this is. This is how life should be. You will probably have ups and downs like most people and every day won't be easy. The good news is that most difficult days will not challenge you as much as you were challenged during your addiction. You will be pleasantly surprised at the inner strength you will be able to harness to ensure victory.

You will be free of the madness.

Conclusion

"Recovery didn't open the gates of heaven and let me in. Recovery opened the gates of hell and let me out." - **Anonymous**

HOPE IS A WONDERFUL feeling, and it doesn't have to end there. Hope is only the springboard to provide you with the excitement and confidence to know that you are worth more than your addiction. When you act on hope, your faith creates change.

With this understanding and belief, using the inner strength you've demonstrated over and over again in dealing with the negative situations you created with your compulsive gambling, with a new can-do mindset, you can overcome your addiction.

But it all comes down to your decision to change your life. My recovery was gradual. I didn't have a gambling experience that made me determined not to gamble again. It was a conscious decision to simply start living a life of being at peace with myself. I no longer wanted to feel shame in my actions, but rather pride.

I wanted to do something big, something I would never have thought I was capable of. I wanted to secure my future where I would only depend on myself and my abilities.

I wanted control.

Once I realized that my fear of change was keeping me from moving forward into the unknown, I was able to take action.

My own recovery involved a 3-step process.

1. Realizing I Was Fearful of Change

2. Changing My Perspective to My Future Self

3. Challenging My GAM Every Time I Was Confronted with the Urge to Gamble

I would like to say at this point, if you experienced real trauma in your life which led to your gambling addiction, this is probably something you need therapy for and you should seek professional advice. You may also want to explore your fears with a counselor so that you can move forward without the excess baggage.

My suggestions and ideas are based solely on my own experience and are not meant in any way to replace the treatment of a true professional.

Realizing I Was Fearful of Change

With this realization I was able to look into what it was I was really afraid of. And I was quite surprised by what I discovered.

I was lazy. I'd never thought of myself in this way before. I'd always held down a job, some reasonably good. My house was always clean and tidy and I cooked homemade meals almost every night.

My laziness related to looking at the effort something would take in order to get the payoff. Because anything worth doing, is worth doing well and that takes effort and commitment. Pressing a button in the casino was much more fun and didn't require any real effort and there was the possibility that a win could happen really fast too. Never mind that it took years and was a complete waste of time and money.

However, instead of commitment which you have control over, it evolved into an addiction with no control and no real payoff.

I also felt that success was somehow for others and not me. I still don't fully understand why I felt this way, but the important point is that I did. I really connected with my spiritual side and in doing so began to feel worthy and loved and with that, I knew that I was here for a purpose and it was time for me to find out what that could possibly be.

For too long I had just accepted my lot and did nothing to create change. Only once I had realized this, did I have the faith in myself and trust in the unknown future to believe there was something better in store for me.

Changing My Perspective to My Future Self

When I envisioned my future self, I saw a successful writer who helped others. It is important to me that you know I have never written a book before. Maybe you could tell this from my writing?

I always knew what I wanted to say to you and I wanted my words to be from the heart. I also wanted to confirm that I could rise to the challenge and deliver something I could be proud of and not let fear of failure or rejection deter me.

This has become my something!

As previously mentioned, you have to manage your expectations and those include those of yourself as well as from the world at large.

As much as I hope this book is well received, it was not written with the goal of becoming a bestselling author.

My next book, *Gambling Addiction Monster*, due out in the fall of 2022, is where I have upped my game.

The journey of success involves constant forward motion, each time building on your previous experience and knowledge, and so I have taken my own advice and challenged myself to not only write and sell a book but to publish a bestselling book.

I will confess that I had brief moments of self-doubt but realized this is perfectly normal when taking steps out of your comfort zone and challenging yourself to do more and be more.

These moments were brief. To be successful, I had to learn as much as possible about writing and publishing and this I did. Only time will tell whether I interpreted everything correctly or not, but it's been fun setting what could be an impossible goal and then tapping into everything within to bring it to life.

I am not suggesting you set out to write a book. I am only suggesting that you find your passion and new purpose, whatever is right for you, and strive to be truly successful with it. It doesn't matter what you do, as long as you feel good about it and makes your life worth living.

If you don't do this and don't feel excited about your life, you could easily relapse and that's the last thing we want.

If I were still gambling today, you would not be reading this!

I am sharing this because I want you to see what is possible after recovery from your gambling addiction.

Anything is possible when you're not gambling. You will finally have a real chance to be a real winner.

Challenging My GAM Every Time I Was Confronted with the Urge to Gamble

When I came up with the GAM concept it was so much easier for me to win those internal battles. My GAM was my Gambling Addiction Monster. This represented my addiction. It was no longer part of me, but rather occupied a part within me.

By separating myself from my GAM, I no longer denied myself the opportunity to gamble as I really didn't want to. I wanted to stop. It was my GAM that wanted me to continue and as my GAM wasn't me, finally getting a grip on the situation was quick. It is far easier to deny something that is not you than to deny yourself. This is, of course, the simplified explanation, but the principle worked for me.

Please believe you can finally be free from your addiction and that you can build a life that is truly worth living. I believe **you can do this**. Now it's *your* chance to believe. All you have to do now is make the conscious decision to commit to your recovery today, and then formulate your own plan to achieve this.

Because, if not now, when?

Thank You

I REALLY APPRECIATE YOU choosing my book to read.

I hope you found the content helpful and that you feel motivated to get started with your own recovery journey.

Could I please ask you to consider posting a review on the Amazon platform?

Your review will help other readers and will support independent authors like myself.

Your feedback will help me to ensure that my books are exactly what readers are looking for and would mean so much to me personally.

Thank you!

References

Antonatos, L. (2021, April 5). *Fear of Change: Causes, Getting Help, & Ways to Cope*.
Choosing Therapy.   Retrieved July 11, 2022.
https://bit.ly/3QgjHBi

Benson, R. (2018, April 25). *The Role of Dopamine in Gambling Withdrawal*. Algamus. Retrieved July 15, 2022.
https://bit.ly/3Q0c81N

Collier, R. (2008, July 15). *Gambling Treatment Options: a role of the dice*. National Library of Medicine.
Retrieved July 17, 2022.
https://bit.ly/3SnS4b4

Fletcher, A. (2020, July 14). *Anne Fletcher Quotes*.
Steps Recovery Centers. Retrieved July 30, 2022.
https://bit.ly/3Q5xbjc

Jones, C. (2020, October 1). *The Impacts of Problem Gambling*. Behavioral Health News.
Retrieved July 17, 2022.
https://bit.ly/3OSdtpV

Julson, MS, RDN, CLT, E. (2022, March 1). *10 Best Ways to Increase Dopamine Levels Naturally*. Healthline.
Retrieved July 9, 2022.
https://bit.ly/3SkNPNw

National Research Council. (1999). *Pathological Gambling: A Critical Review*. The National Academies Press.
Retrieved July 28, 2022.
https://bit.ly/3Qgqv1A

Roizman, T. (2018, November 27). *Chocolate & Dopamine*. SFGate. Retrieved July 24, 2022.
https://bit.ly/3zu1AAR

Slutske, W. S. (2006, February 1). *Natural Recovery and Treatment-Seeking in Pathological Gambling: Results of Two U.S. National Surveys*.
The American Journal of Psychiatry.
Retrieved July 21, 2022.
https://bit.ly/3OWcuVI

Stuck, A. M. (2021, June 3). *Fear of the Unknown: Causes, Signs, & How to Overcome*.
Choosing Therapy. Retrieved July 29, 2022.
https://bit.ly/3oQssGw